# Her Time To Speak

*A Collection of Spoken*

*Word Poetry on*

*Self Love,*

*Relationships,*

*Encouragement,*

*and Life*

By Amber LaMotte

## Dedication

This one is for every person who struggles with letting their voice be heard and the pressure of pleasing others.

Please God with your gifts and talents. Be strong and courageous letting Him use you.

# Acknowledgements

I take this moment to give glory, honor, and praise to the Most High God for allowing me to accomplish this goal of writing and publishing my first poetry book. Without Him, I wouldn't be able to do this at all. He is the reason I write the way I do, whether it's to encourage others or to be able to present something that shows others I can relate to them. Most of all I want to present a level of authenticity that reveals that I am human. We all have a purpose and story to tell in our own way. Thank you Heavenly Father for blessing me with this gift and talent. I will continue to use them for your glory, to reach those you have called for your kingdom.

Every person that's ever encouraged me to reach for my dreams, the desires of my heart, thank you! This is only the beginning. Thank you for believing in me and for showing constant support.

I give special thanks to my two adorable little girls who love just about anything that I do or write. I hope this encourages you to reach for whatever desires God has placed in your hearts without giving up. Don't ever bury them. Use them for God's glory always. Thank you for just existing which makes me want to become greater each day for the both of you. Love mommy!

# Table Of Contents

Her Time To Speak

# Self Love

*Personally, Culturally, and Purposefully*

*"You won't always be everyone's cup of tea. Just be sure to be God's cup of tea, intentionally."*

*-Amber L.*

### *I Like Me*

You may not like the way I talk

but I like me.

You may not like the way I walk

but I like me.

You may not like the way I think

but I like me.

You may not like the way I dress

but I like me.

You may not like the way I sing

but I like me.

You may not like the way I believe

but I like me.

You may not like the way I embrace

but I like me.

You may not like the scars on my face

but I like me.

You may not like my hair

but I like me.

You may not like the way I share my gifts

but I like me.

You may not like my skin, tone, or shade

but I like me,

and I'm not worried or afraid

about you not accepting anything to mighty

for you to perceive,

because truth is,

it's for the lost sheep.

God gets the glory.

So,

for anyone out there who

the devil has ever tried to silence,

stand up and tell your story.

Who needs man's validation

if God has already approved?

Be strong and courageous

letting Him use you

to move hearts to be

reconciled back unto Him.

-Amber L.

*"Always include God in your decision making process with relationships"*

*-Amber L.*

## *Nobody's Fool*

Girl,

who told you to

volunteer yourself as

a transplant,

trying to fit in a place

where you don't belong.

You will never be

flesh of his flesh,

bone of his bone.

You picked this guy when

God said "WRONG"

"MISSION ABORT",

while you were steady saying,

uhhn uhhn God,

"IGNORE",

sweeping those red flags

under the rug at your door,

continuing on with him

trying to build rapport,

even though he was

just not that into you

but saw the extent

you would go to

just to be with him,

and in return,

making you a puppet

he could use.

Don't you ever play

NOBODY'S FOOL!


You are worth so much

more than that,

far above rubies.

He's probably used to

cubic zirconia,

lab made imitating stones.

A real one will dig

for your treasure,

no matter how hard it is

once he realizes he's

in the right zone.

So, chin up sis.

Fix your crown.

Reverse that frown

and don't ever again

give it away to a man

acting like a clown.

-Amber L.

*"Never think you have to dim another woman's light in order for yours to shine"*

*-Amber L.*

## *Insecurities*

I appreciate people who are genuine,

down to Earth,

those comfortable in their own skin,

who don't try to

patronize others,

whose beauty glows from within,

as if it's a sin to love oneself.

Those who aren't,

INSECURITIES are loud.

Sis, they are screaming

for help.

What is it that you hate

so much about the next sister?

Is it her skin,

her complexion or

how she gracefully be flexing

confidence,

the dominance in showing

others how to be yourself?

Her resilience?

The level of brilliance she

ascends to when being creative?

What is it?

Because in all these things

mentioned,

I still can't figure out where the hate

is stemmed from.

Maybe it's because you feel

like a slouch

or you come from the slums,

mistakenly judging her

drawing a conclusion that

she is spoon fed

and don't understand the struggle

you come from.

Maybe it's your weight

and you feel at a disadvantage

when it comes to finding a mate

because you think most of

these men want nothing to do with your curves

unless you're a size eight,

nothing more,

everything less.

Or maybe it's because

you see that she is blessed,

a highly favored woman,

with God and man,

comparing yourself to her

like your Creator won't beautify

your life with His plans.


What is it?

You are looking a mess.

All the things hidden in your heart are

unveiled and confessed

every time you open your mouth

so pressed about the next,

tearing down instead of building up

but closing your mouth with feigned love.


I think you should do some dissecting

and stop neglecting what's

broken on the inside

instead of playing

master of disguise,

trying to hide behind lies

that only pacify your

insecurities.

Deal with the pride.

Deal with the rejection.

Deal with the hate, the envy, jealousy

and depression.

Deal with the fact that

you feel you're not good enough

because you don't know self love.


Tend to your wounds

before they consume you.

If you don't,

they will only resurface

everytime you're in the presence

of a woman who knows

what her worth is.

Then,

that hateful spirit will once again

use you.

-Amber L.

*"When you begin to love yourself you develop a zero tolerance for the lack of love from anyone else."*

*-Amber L.*

## *Self Love*

Self love is,

you will not disrespect me.

Neglecting won't be tolerated.

I don't have to suffer

your abuse of my love

until I'm finally

appreciated.

Self love is,

no one is going to tell me

that I'm not good enough

ever again.

I refused to be something I'm not.

My natural beauty is still in

just like real hip hop.


Self love is,

separating myself from all things

detrimental to my health,

mentally, physically, spiritually,

and staying up until three,

finding my release lyrically,

writing poetry because it's therapy.

-Amber L.

*"Dear beautiful black girl, your hair defies gravity and speaks for you when you enter the room. Let it speak powerful things."*

*-Amber L.*

## *Queen of Shade*

I want my hair so big that

I become the queen of shade.

I am fearfully and wonderfully made.

You could never make me

hate my natural.

This afro is going to steal the

spotlight,

be the only thing visible

in your eyesight.

Don't try to make me

tame her either.

I can decipher from

the little snooty remarks of

"you not gone comb your hair",

or the way you just stop and stare.

Uhn uhn..

Don't you dare judge me.

Don't be angry cus

I'm a phenomenal woman

from my head down to my feet.

I know you caught a whiff

of that sweet aroma of

coconut milk, mango butter,

and jamaican black castor oil,

which keeps my hair

oh so moisturized,

shining and in the perfect coils.

My curls are popping.

Haters be blocking,

trying to make us hate us but

I'm the queen of shade.

                              -Amber L.

*"My brother, my father, my friend, be vigilant because we need you. No one's going to have your backs the way that we do."*

*-Amber L.*

## *Black Men Are*

Black men are the sun in the blue sky,

the moon at night.

Black men are either a chocolate high or a caramel delight.

Black men are intelligent.

Black men are relevant to society.

Black men are kings, priests, or dynasties.

Black men are the ships that

are victims to piracy.

Black men are our anxiety.

Hands up. Don't shoot. I can't breathe.

Black men are the so called strange fruit

that just mysteriously gets found

hanging from a tree.

Black men are the rhymes and beats.

Black men are the perfect pitch to our melodies.

Black men are security.

Black men are inferiority,

now, historically, and until Jesus' second coming.

Black men are everything.

Black men are appreciated,

even though they are

the world's most hated.

-Amber L.

*"Own who you are and don't be sorry."*

*Amber L.*

## Unapologetic Black Woman

I am an

unapologetic black woman

No,

I don't have an attitude.

Betty Wright told me,

you can't show your teeth

to every guy you meet,

but I think she meant person.

Don't worsen the divide

coming over here with that

team lightskin

team darkskin

pride.

I believe we're all

Queens.

A satin hair bonnet

is one of our most prized

accessories.

Oh yeah, and we love our

chicken wings,

hot, lemon pepper,

ALL FLATS please.

Don't forget the ranch

or blue cheese.

Did I mention the cornbread

and collard greens?

Seasoned!

We add the taste to everything,

the reason it's not bland,

from our food

to our moves,

down to the rhythm and blues.

We are multi-talented,

multi-faceted,

dripping in melanin ,

committing sin

just in the beauty of

our presence.

sincerely,

an unapologetic black

woman.

-Amber L.

*Brown skin girl, don't let the world admire you and then not have a clue of how beautiful you are.*

*- Amber L.*

## Beautiful Brown Girl

Beautiful brown girl with your

kinks and your curls,

dripping in melanin,

admired by the world,

the epitome of brilliance,

known for your strength

and your resilience,

a breathtaking sight,

fearfully and wonderfully made

in the image of Christ,

Soak in this moment.

You definitely have

bragging rights.


I'm speaking to my sisters

and all the queens

and although this poem

is about us,

I haven't forgotten about

our handsome kings.

I had to take a moment

just to honor us

because learning to love

ourselves is a crucial must.

I know most may think that

in order to be beautiful

that you NEED your bundles

and your lashes,

but take a look at the rest

of the world,

taking injections

just to get your lips

and your .....

Thought I was about to curse

Huh.

I'm just keeping it real

beautiful brown girl,

you are the real deal.


It doesn't matter if

you're short tall skinny or thick.

Don't look at these celebrities

and think their bodies are "it".

It doesn't matter if

you are light skin, brown skin,

or dark skin.

Outwardly, you still have it

going on.

Now balance it with the beauty

that's within.


Pluck up your westernized

thinking

and return to your roots.

If you don't know where to start,

come to me and

I'll school you.

Let's be clear,

I'm talking about care.

We learned how to manage

every other style

except our natural hair.


The bottom line is,

the way God made us

is perfectly fine.

To think there's a flaw with

how you look

is absurd.

That explains why master

wanted a piece of something

so divine.


Beautiful brown girl

I'm your sister and you're mine.

Let's not envy and hate

one another.

Learn how to embrace

and uplift in time.


You are unique,

peculiar.

There's no one else on this Earth

that could be you.

Only someone attempting to

look familiar.

So, to your natural appearance,

always stay true.

Beautiful brown girl,

That's you and that's me.

The next time you take a

look in the mirror,

tell yourself you're beautiful

and believe.


For all my sisters that use

things to enhance your beauty,

don't miss what I'm saying,

you're still a cutie.

I'm just trying to get us to see

that your natural beauty

is all that you need.

-Amber L.

# *Relationships*

*In General*

*"Relationships thrive with trust, integrity, and authenticity".*

*-Amber L.*

## Safe Haven

Are you a vault

or a vending machine,

a safe haven,

or are my deepest

and darkest secrets

in jeopardy?

A parody

is your favorite sitcom,

not the fragile,

vulnerable parts of my life.

Don't make fun.

Don't run and tell that.

Prove your loyalty

to me.

Let me know you got

my back,

without stabbing.

It's happened,

one too many times.

I put my guard up

cus' I don't want to

flatline.

Divine is the love

I disseminate.

My expectation of those

I allow in

is to reciprocate and cultivate

a now formed bond

where we both feel safe,

not the kind where

they smile in your face.

Shout out to the O'Jays,

giving you praise

all the while hating,

translation,

the wrong relations.

Carnival Sensation

is the only ship

I want to be on

having fun with

genuine,

trustworthy,

loved ones.

-Amber L.

*"Cry for a moment but only for a moment. Then, quickly find your happy place again."*

*-Amber L.*

## Washed Memories

One time I ate ice cream

for breakfast, lunch,

and dinner the entire week.

Then, stayed up the whole

night.

I couldn't sleep.

I had you on my mind,

trying to figure out

how much time it would

take just to get over you.

I cried a sea;

enough tears to fill the world

and wash away the memories

of you and me.

-Amber L.

*"Effective communication of anything requires reciprocation."*

*-Amber L.*

## Essence of Life

Today I made some tea.

There was a message

for me.

It read,

"the essence of life

is to communicate love",

but I find that

the world is hard of hearing.

We can speak love fluently

but it's still not enough

for those caught up

in their selfish ambitions

and if it's not their language,

then they're definitely

not listening.


Love sounds like

someone checking on you

making sure you're fine,

when there's so much

you have to do

in little to no time.

It sounds like,

someone willing to

fast and pray with you

to help get victory

in that fight.

It sounds like,

giving someone credit

where it is due,

respecting their copyrights.

It sounds like,

all the secrets you share

are safe with me.

I won't try to expose you

just because I'm angry.

It sounds like

giving you the clothes

off my back,

even if it's my last.

You don't have to ask.

It sounds like,

when you're not feeling

alright,

pick up the phone

and call me.

I don't care if it's

in the evening at six

or in the morning at three.


Love is always

communicated.

Self absorption

and trauma keeps it

from being received

and reciprocated.

-Amber L.

*"Every rejection propels you in the right direction for acceptance".*

*-Amber L.*

## Sting Of Rejection

I can write a book

when I'm feeling blue.

I try my best to

shake off this mood.

My attitude

can get very rude.

I just want to be

close to you,

in your company.

The rejection hurts.

It stings,

and the only way

to cure the pain

is to write poetry

or sing.


Let the music flow

through my soul,

every lyric,

every note.

You're poison to me

and this is my only antidote.

-Amber L.

*"Identify a tree by its fruit and you will never be fooled"*

*-Amber L.*

## Forbidden Fruit

They say the blacker

the berry

the sweeter the juice.

What's sweet about

forbidden fruit?

You're poison,

even though you say

you're a boysenberry.

From the outer appearance,

I can distinctively see

you're a Jerusalem Cherry,

too toxic for me.

I consumed you

and received an

irregular heartbeat.

I was deceived,

expecting a corrupt tree

to turn out to be

something good for me,

devastated from your

disloyalty.

I felt the effects

of your solanine;

sick to my stomach

with gastrointestinal infections

and cramping.

I played the fool.

These are the side effects

of eating forbidden fruit.

- Amber L.

*"Sow the seeds of love."*

*-Amber L.*

## *What Is Love: Part two*

LOVE.

We all want to know it

but to know love

is to show it.

So, the question is,

what are you sowing?

Whatever seeds you plant

will start growing,

bringing in a harvest

of what you are holding

inside.

Don't let it be

hatred, pride, or strife,

giving satan legal rights

in your life

to come in to kill,

steal, and destroy.

Oh boy!

We reap what we sow.


I'll tell you a story

about a man that I know,

the perfect example

of how love should go,

the lover of my soul.

This man,

loved me when I

didn't love myself.

He cared for me anytime

I was in distress needing

help,

even though

I hadn't fully confessed

Him.

He said you are mine

giving me time

so I could get it together,

backsliding yet

still being my peace

within the weather.

I have never known

a love like this before;

one who laid down

His life for me,

extending grace,

knocking on the

doors of my heart,

who would come in

and sup with me

just as long as I

chose to be set apart.


You see,

love is sacrifice.

It is rising to different

heights to put others

before self.

It is extending help

to the poor and needy,

the widowed and bereaving,

the oppressed,

bringing them justice.

It is loving your neighbor

as yourself.

You don't want it done

to you,

then don't do it to me.

There is no partiality,

no hypocrisy in love.

It is rejoicing when your

sister or brother rejoices.

It is tuning out that little

envious or jealous voice

that tries to creep up

inside because if He

did it for your neighbor,

then you know that

He's outside,

in your neighborhood,

which means that

it's almost your time.

It is the greatest

commandment from the

Divine,

that vine in which we

all should abide

if we expect to receive

eternal life.

It is overlooking strife

created by others,

going by another name

charity,

that covers a multitude

of sins.

Anymore questions about

what love is?


We all want to know it

but to know love

is to show it.

So,

the question is,

what are you sowing?

Whatever seeds you plant

will start growing,

bringing in a harvest

of what you are

holding inside.

Let the seeds of love

reign in your life .

-Amber L.

*"Cutting the strings means taking back your power when taken for granted."*

*-Amber L.*

## Strings

She was the object

of his affection,

literally an object.

How obnoxious it was.

He thought he could

just pick her up,

play with her

when he was bored,

then put her away

temporarily,

yet still keeping

her on his cord.

Like the strings on

a guitar,

he played and plucked

with her heart.

and if her attachment to him

began to loosen up,

he quickly gave her

a tune up.

-Amber L.

*"Some stories are our greatest teachers. Discover the gems in it."*

*-Amber L.*

## *If I Was To Write A Love Poem*

If I was to write a love poem,

it would go something like this.

I know you have many

options to choose from,

but only invest your time

in to woo one.

Why have I found favor

in your sight?

I'd approach you

like the king you are

just to find out why

I've ravished your heart.

It would happen at

a divine time.

My beloved will say

"You are mine",

and I'd know that I'm his.

Like Esther,

I'd be prepared

so I wouldn't miss

a time such as this.

I'd suddenly go from

being your sister,

to your love,

to your spouse,

from a mediocre lifestyle

into your royal house.

Like Rebekah,

I'd go with no questions asked.

I'd be your Ruth

while you be my Boaz.

We'd be intertwined.

You'd cover me with your love,

serving me with fine wine

made from the choicest vine.

I'd be sure not to idolize

but in my eyes,

you'd be my lord,

ready to draw your sword

against anyone who crosses

the borders of your queen.

I'd stay in your field

always helping you yield

much fruit,

be right there to help uproot,

planting all over again,

bringing in a bigger

return of investment.

If I was to write a love poem,

it would go something like this.

-Amber L.

*"There's an old saying that says, you have to pay the cost to be the boss."*

*-Amber L.*

## Submission Activated

They say black women

don't like to submit,

which I can admit

sometimes it's true.

We like to wear the pants

and show how independent

we are without you.

This only applies to a few.


On the other hand,

some women will do

whatever we can for

the one who is truly a man.

The submission will come easily

because he protects provides

and is able to lead his family.

She can trust him to handle

his business

because she's witnessed

that he's ambitious

plus consistent.

His decisions are not selfish,

making sure she's secure

being selfless,

making it impossible for her

to be rebellious.

His actions line up with his words

because he loves her,

you know,

an action verb,

not just empty words.


Some men,

well boys,

think that a woman should

automatically be submissive

since physically he's the man.

Okay.

Give her something

she can submit to.

She can't do that if

she's forced to wear the pants,

especially if he's had

the chance time and time again

to show that he can

protect provide and lead

but chooses everytime

to neglect her needs,

being unavailable emotionally.


Some men say that

it's the woman's fault.

She won't let him lead,

making us the scapegoat

but I disagree.


The Lord has placed

something inside of you,

making it easy to

take authority.

This is not done by force

or control

but by knowing your role,

being an Ephesians five man,

nourishing

and cherishing her

as his own soul.

Some just choose to refuse

to tap into it,

being filled with excessive

testosterone,

ruling as tyrants and misogynist.


What do you guys really want?

Someone you can rule

and control,

or someone who will

help you meet your goal?


Grievous words stir up anger

and a lack of trust in someone

that's supposed to be the head,

makes a woman feel like

she's in imminent danger,

causing her to improvise

just so she can survive.


So,

the next time you talk

about how a woman won't

submit,

do a self check

of your character

and see what part

you play in it,

because I believe submission

is a trait instilled in us

from our Creator.

It just takes the correct man

to activate.

Let it resonate.

-Amber L.

*"Trauma bonding is throwing "love" on wounds intentionally created".*

*-Amber L.*

## *What's Love...Got To Do*

What's love got to do

with your inconsistency,

the distance you create

between you and me,

the dreams you are selling,

the way you bleed on

someone who isn't responsible

for your hurt.

What's love got to do

with you treating me

like dirt?

-Amber L.

.

# Life Experiences And Encouragement

*"I surrendered."*

*-Amber L.*

## Desires

I thought I knew what I wanted.

In fact,

what I wanted was all that I could see.

Lord please forgive me for my idolatry.

I no longer want what I want

but what you say is best for me.

The desires of my heart,

my destiny,

will line up with your perfect will for me.

Conceived,

while I was still in my mother's womb.

All of the derails and details

of my complicated life

was only making room,

grooming this seed,

for my blossoming and blooming,

preparing me to be all that

you've called me to be.

-Amber L.

*"You are enough. You are fearfully and wonderfully made and you are more than a conqueror through Christ who strengthens you."*

*-Amber L.*

## Stand

There have been times

where I have been

made to feel like

I wasn't enough,

like I'm too much

too outspoken

too opinionated

too confident

too dominant

too strong for a woman

too assertive

too introverted

too at peace with me

too happy

too genuinely sweet

too tall of a tree

rooted in God deeply

too honest with this poetry

and I was,

and probably still am

but one thing I will continue to do is

STAND.

I will stand as my Creator

holds my hand and speak

when He leads me.

I will stand and help

strengthen the weak.

I will stand speaking

life to the diseased,

bringing them healing.

I will stand and expose the deceit,

respectfully.

Life and death are in the power

of the tongue.

I won't run even if I'm shunned.

No more concealing

who I am inside

just to keep folks satisfied.

I'm a daughter of Zion,

of a King ,

the Tribe of Judah,

who is also a lion.

I will stand because

there is no denying

the gifts the Lord

has given me.

Being an unprofitable servant

is not my destiny,

or being cast out

into outer darkness

where there is weeping

and gnashing of teeth

because I allowed fear

and what people think to

get to me.

I will stand with love

even when I'm hated

or when haters go out

their way to make sure

I feel humiliated.

It's not my fight.

Vengeance is the Lord's

and he will repay it.

So, be careful with me

because when I stand,

you may perceive that

I'm alone

when actually I'm

surrounded by an army,

a host of angels,

that will bind,

shut up, and seal your

fallen three

at the powerful commands,

the words I speak.


You might ask,

where does my boldness

come from?

And I'll look you in the face

telling you,

His Son.

-Amber L.

*"We are misunderstood to those we are not called to."*

*-Amber L.*

## Uninteresting Book

We judge the things that

we don't take the time

to understand,

but demand with an

open hand,

the golden rule,

to be our critic's

measuring tool

against what others find

to be rare in ourselves.

We expect folks to

remain closed up

like an uninteresting book,

on a shelf that collects dust

because we can't trust

if it suits us

based on the appearance.

Didn't you ever learn

to not judge a book by

it's cover?

It's how you end up

missing out,

leaving room for another

to discover the gems,

the treasure,

in the depths of the pages

of that perceived to be

uninteresting book.

-Amber L.

*"God will disrupt your plans for His plans for your life. Make sure you're aligned."*

*-Amber L.*

## His Will

I know the place I was in

was for God to capture

my undivided attention.

Sometimes you have to be

isolated from everything else

in order for God to get you

to listen.

He knows what that

reason is.

This is a journey that

I had to walk next

to God with

and in the midst of it,

He was cleaning me up

opening my eyes,

giving me no choice

but to submit to

His will for my life.

-Amber L.

*"Being slow to speak keeps you from being put to shame."*

*-Amber L.*

## *Don't Open Your Mouth Against Me*

Don't open your mouth

against me.

You don't know me man.

My Creator is the one

that fashioned me.

I am the works of His hands.

Whatever goes on

in my life is His plan,

whether that's so

He gets the victory

or to reprimand me.

You can't judge a book

by it's cover.

And any secrets shared

should not be discovered

by another,

talebearing, gossiping, backbiting,

saying you love God

but hating your brother,

sisters too.

You can kill folks everyday

just by the words you say.

He said keep His commandments.

Thou shall not kill

or is that one less that

you have to obey?

Don't open your mouth

against me.

Just because you see

the rain and the wind

beating against me

doesn't mean I'm guilty.

What's filthy is

the mind that have

the time to mind my

business.

The Lord will deal with

anyone who tries to

bear false witness.

Do you have some

receipts?

Deceit can come

out of the mouth

of anyone,

rolling fluently

down a hater's tongue.


Don't open your mouth

against me.

I haven't always made

decisions that are holy

but don't hold me to

a manner of behavior

I've already repented from,

especially if it came by way

of a stumbling block

through some.

You see,

the way satan works is,

he constantly reminds you

of your offenses

through his minions

and your shortcomings,

so you will be filled with

guilt, shame, humiliation,

and be less forthcoming

for the most high.

He is the accuser of the

brethren.

The father of lies.

Surprise! surprise! surprise!

I shall live and not die.

I have victory through Christ.

Don't open your mouth

against me.

-Amber L.

*"In the end, the underdogs win."*

*-Amber L.*

## Dark Horse

They watch me,

closely observing.

I'm placed under scrutiny.

Their thoughts are,

"It's impossible for her

to take the lead".

They don't believe

in me.

Looks can be very

deceiving.

Little about me is known,

which makes me

prone to losing

in their eyes.

My coat is the perfect

disguise for what I hold

inside.

On the flip side,

I'm actually trained to go

but you'll never know

because you prematurely

cast your vote.

You're most comfortable

with the status quo.

They must have missed

this year's memo.

The dark horses,

the underdogs,

the Cinderellas,

the Esthers,

will break the mold

and I don't care about

what you've been

told before.

These are the ones who

will spread their wings

like eagles and soar,

unexpectedly.

The dark horse

does a clean sweep

of those keeping score,

triumphing.

Don't be so quick to

count out the least likely.

-Amber L.

*"It takes up too much energy to hate on someone. I choose love."*

*-Amber L.*

## Disease

I have power to love you

from a distance.

I have power to not be

offended by your spirit.

I have power to not

hold any grudges against you.

I have power to call on

the help to raise up a standard

against the hate you spew.

I have power to be true,

even when their is malice

and guile in everything you do.

I have power to be kind,

even though I know the

reason you can't look me

in the eyes.

I have power to be

everything I need to be

to those who despise me

openly or secretly.

But what I don't have is,

time,

time for the spirit of jealousy.

I will let you be.

That disease is deadly

and I want to live,

physically, spiritually, and mentally.

I can't be around anyone

that will try to shoot me

literally or figuratively.

However,

I will gladly petition

on your behalf

for healing and victory,

to overcome that stronghold

possessing a beautiful

innocent soul

because I know

you're not to be of that

wicked one who possessed

Cain

but of the Lord's fold.

I want you to know that

I don't hate you.

I love you.

But love never gains the

approval of jealousy.

So,

I'm praying for you.

                    -Amber L.

*"Choose right the first time because there may not be a second.*

*-Amber L.*

## *Red or Blue*

I'm the red pill

that you find in the matrix

but you'd rather take the blue,

basic,

avoiding complexity

since it forces you

to face the truth of reality.

I understand

your mentality is set on

the things that are

mediocre,

lacks luster,

doesn't shine.

Your self esteem

slowly diminished over time.

So,

you overlook

what's fine and exceptional,

choosing what's comfortable,

but what's comfortable

is not always what's

expedient.

Blue pill or red pill,

they have different ingredients.

Which will you choose?

Win with the truth

or lose with what's inexpedient,

the blue.

Whichever you do

is what you have to live with.

There will not be another

option between the two.

-Amber L.

*"Pain is a part of the process".*

*-Amber L.*

## Four Letter Word

Pain

is that other

four letter word.

It hurts.

It can bring out the

worst in you.

Pain can cause you

to change once you

bear it long enough.

Pain can cause you

to go insane,

even check out of this

game of life.

You feel it the most

at night.

Tears of sorrow fill

your bed.

Your head is clouded

and now you doubt it

that anyone would

be able to get close

to your heart ever again

because so called friends

family, and ex lovers

have pulled back

the dart,

released it and torn

you apart until you're

left with the scars of

betrayal, rejection,

and abandonment.

You name it.

Different seeds were

sowed and I reaped

this four letter word

a hundredfold,

but the one who

molded me

won't allow me to

sink into pity.

In fact,

in pain I've

found my purpose.

I never would have

known what my worth is

except it had been for

this four letter word.

In pain I've learned

my lessons.

Some things are not

worth addressing.

Just turn the page

and don't look back.

I no longer want to

pick up the slack of

those who chose

to mishandle me.

In pain

I've learned to

bless my enemies

and pray for those who

despitefully used me.

In pain

I've learned not

to beg for anyone's

help.

The one up above

has a love for me

that is unchanging.

I see it daily as I'm

remaining in Him.

In pain,

I've learned forgiveness.

I won't constantly remind

you of what your offense is

but back back back back

and give me 50 feet

if you're unrepentant.

So much can be recalled

of this four letter word.

I bet when ya'll heard

the title,

ya'll thought it was about

that action verb,

love,

which is clearly something

you can feel like you

do too much of.

That's the reason why

I'm able to write about

that other four letter word

in the first place.

-Amber L.

*"Down to earth is the best way to be, full of humility."*


*-Amber L.*

## Earthly

The best people in the world

are the ones down to Earth,

closer to dirt than the sky,

because when most get their wings

or become an eagle,

they are overtaken by a spirit

of pride.

They may try to conceal it

with false humility,

a composure full of tranquility,

until the cover is blown.

Then there's exposure to

who they really are

under the surface.

They rise and then begin

to look down on those beneath them

as if they are worthless.

A title is only a title.

We all have a purpose.

We may not all reach the sky.

Some are made specifically

for the surface where the turf is,

but still,

they shall not be despised,

because they are still

fearfully and wonderfully made

in our Creator's eyes,

the only one who is allowed

to look down on us but sits high.


The same ones who are lowly,

are the ones that Jesus wants.

The meek will inherit the Earth.

Thy kingdom come,

not those who are

haughty, high-minded

humiliating others and

putting on fronts for validation

from the world.


Without the Earthly,

those that have reached some height,

really wouldn't be worth much.

That favor comes from

God and man.

Without both,

there is plenty they wouldn't be

able to touch.


You can ascend and then descend

for being condescending to others.

God will be the one who removes you

setting up another.

My brother, my sister,

be careful how you treat people.

Never forget where you once begin.

because at some point we've all had

humble beginnings.

-Amber L.

*"In isolation is where strength and character is built."*

*-Amber L.*

## My Wilderness

They say seasons come

and seasons go

but I've been stuck in the desert.

There's no pleasure,

only parched weather.

Tumbleweeds is the only

company rolling through.

I'm in a desolate place.

My own kindred has

hidden their faces from me.

I've been abased.

I cry for help

but no one's listening.

My name is dragged

through the mud

by my enemies.

Who's defending me?

Satan has conquered

and divided.

Used to be friends

are seeming more like

frenemies.

In their eyes

I must be guilty

wicked or filthy,

and think they have

the right to judge me

because they've seen

my flaws,

but won't do righteous

judgement to those

actually breaking laws.

They see my condition

and use it as ammunition

to hurt me,

being discouraging.


The truth is,

the Lord brought me

to a secret place ,

my wilderness,

to be purged

and planted,

to become a

tree of righteousness,

producing fruit with

much tenderness.

It hasn't been an

easy process.

I was almost overtaken

by bitterness,

and unforgiveness.

The Most High put me

through the fire so I

could be a witness.

I realized this.

To the cry of Joseph,

I can relate.

The way Daniel was

left in the lion's den

for dead,

my life was at stake.

Help was only an option

through oppression.

It was not up for debate.

The misogyny became

disgusting.

I became distrusting

of men that's supposed

to be of God

and of the bias.

Frankly,

my attitude from there on

was they can kiss my

hot cross buns.

I knew that wasn't how

I should run.

I wanted to give up.

From the very moment

I gave my life completely

over to God,

the warfare was tough.

Where's the love?


The Lord taught me

a lesson.

Quit looking for a blessing

or affection from man.

Trust in the one who

have the power to withhold

and to open His hand,

abundantly.

Life confronted me

for making flesh my arm.

My faith was increased

the further I got into

my wilderness

and I saw no harm.

Everything I needed

was provided.

I confided in Him

first,

believed,

then streams

of water flowed into

my life,

right when I felt

at my wits end.

Every now and then,

He would throw in

little blessings,

filling me with hope.

I would keep pressing.

He gave me a glimpse

of my promised land,

the plans He have for me,

my peace,

where evil and adversity

must cease,

my expected end.

What a friend I have

in Jesus.

We must seek

and search for Him

with our whole heart.

The one with the power

to make the Red Sea

part,

even start making ways

in our wilderness,

rivers in the deserts.

The measure of grace

given to me

is what helped get me

through this place,

my wilderness.

                    -Amber L.

## Author's Notes

When I was in my adolescent years, somewhere between middle school and high school, I discovered I had the gift of poetry. It first started with me writing songs in a book that I would dread for anyone to read. If we ever had an assignment in English class on poetry, I would always do well because it came natural to me, plus, I loved it. For a period of time, I buried this talent for numerous reasons, one being fear and another of not really knowing my worth at the time.

"Her Time To Speak", is a collection of spoken word poems that are empowering, sassy, encouraging, and rooted in real life experiences or seasons. I use my gift and whatever God places on my heart in attempts to connect with others, giving them something they can relate to, learn from, overcome, and most of all be reconciled back to God.

Each time I write a poem, I literally ask God to give me the words because I know whatever He gives to me will be powerful, I also know that the different seasons and chapters of life we go through can help someone else if we allow our voices to be heard. God allows us to go through different things for His glory. He gets the glory through your testimony of how you overcame those obstacles and in whichever way he chooses to use you. Some of these poems are a direct reflection of experiences in my life, from my early twenties to my mid twenties. I know I have plenty of experiences to go through as I become older but for now and up until this point, I share pieces of those experiences and what I've learned from them with you, as well as the strength of overcoming. Let's just say I'm no longer in the mind frame of what I was in at the time some of these experiences occurred.

Her Time To Speak